So... You Want to Get Well?

The Disparities in Mental Health Treatment

Fred Long

Certified Psychiatric Rehabilitation Practitioner

Certified Peer Specialist

Certified Whole Health Coach

ISBN-13:
978-1494712518

ISBN-10:
1494712512

DEDICATION

This work is dedicated to the mental health patients I have been privileged to serve and to know over the past decade. My wish is that you may find the peace you deserve and learn to live life in a more satisfying way. Recovery from your diagnosis is not impossible. I am also dedicating this work to all those mental health professionals I have worked alongside. This work is not to insult you, but to open your eyes.

ACKNOWLEDGMENTS

My thanks to Dr. Daniel Trussell; Sue Marlowe of NAMI; Dr. Robert Prehn, CEO of The Bradley Center; Tim Browning, IT professional; for their feedback while writing this book. A special thanks is given to the many people (patients, staff and psychiatrists) who assisted me in my quest to find myself.

Foreword:

Mental health should be one of the top priorities in research, funding, and in the minds of the people of the United States of America; unfortunately, it has not achieved this importance. Much improvement has been made regarding mental health in recent years; however, there is much more that needs to be done. When you consider one in four people in the United States will experience mental illness during the coming year, you can see how important an issue mental health has become.

A recovery model of mental health care has even evolved, but within state mental hospitals no attention is being paid to this method of treating people with mental disorders. Many clinicians have not been trained in this model of mental health care and more than a few clinicians the author has known are not aware that such a model exists.

While it is true that people with mental illnesses are no longer chained to hospital walls, the treatment these people are still receiving is an insult to them and to humanity. This book will explore some of the disparity of treatment taking place in regards to the mentally ill.

Table of Contents:

Part One: The Maze of Mental Illness

Part Two: Maneuvering Through the Maze of Mental Illness

Part One:

The Maze of Mental Illness

A Brief History

Unfair treatment toward the mentally ill in the United States has been around a long time. As the first colonies were being formed, people with mental health problems were thought possessed by a demon or by the devil. They were subsequently chained and sometimes beaten. Often they were placed in seclusion where they would languish until death. In these places, the mentally ill would be without restroom facilities and food. If they were not committed to an institution their families would lock them in cellars or attics because they were considered to be a disgrace to the family.

This type of treatment persisted until around 1840 when Dorothea Dix began to lobby for reform in mental health. She would eventually visit Europe and talk with the Pope of that day in an attempt to convince him to examine how poorly the mentally ill were being treated throughout the world.

In the late 1800's, Nelly Bly, a reporter for a prominent New York newspaper, posed as a mental patient. Her articles helped get more money for mental institutions, but did little to change the way people thought of others who had a mental illness. Also, during this time state mental hospitals became overcrowded and treatment of the mentally ill did not improve. Food for the patients in these hospitals often contained worms and was unfit to eat.

Clifford Beers, a former mental patient, wrote an autobiography in the early 1900's that detailed his experiences of feeling degraded and dehumanized while in a mental hospital in Connecticut. He formed an organization that later became known as the National Mental Health Association.

The use of drugs, shock therapy, and prefrontal lobotomy began in the 1930's. These treatments would eventually prove to be as dehumanizing as being chained to the wall of a dungeon and having to urinate on the floor.

The 1940's ushered in the advent of powerful psychotropic drugs like Thorazine. These medications would prove beneficial to patients; however, their side effects would cause patients to stop taking them as soon as they were released from the state hospital.

With the next decade, psychiatric hospitals showed a significant increase in numbers. In 1955, there were over a half million patients in state mental hospitals. This overcrowding meant that patients did not receive the proper attention needed to ensure the most beneficial care.

During the 1960's the deinstitutionalization of mental hospitals began. The problem with this was that even the most severely mental ill people were discharged. These people soon became homeless and even more mentally ill because of lack of treatment and proper medication.

In 1999, two long term residents of Georgia's mental health establishment filed a suit against Georgia under the American with Disabilities Act. Louis Carter and Elizabeth Wilson eventually had to take their case to the Supreme Court. The Supreme Court made a decision which is now known as the *Olmstead Decision.* The two women who filed this suit only wanted to be released from the state hospital. They had both been long term patients (almost their whole lives) and felt they should be free. The *Olmstead Decision* brought freedom to these two ladies and thousands more like them. However, Georgia ranks among the lowest of the states in implementing this decision. Thus, many long term patients still await their freedom from mental institutions in the State of Georgia.

Since the 1960's there hasn't been much progress in the way the mentally ill are treated. Of course there have been significant improvements in the medications developed for the mentally ill, but the way mental health professionals and hospitals still regard people with a mental health diagnosis has not shown any marked improvement. The history of the treatment of the mentally ill has proven itself to be one whose past is not reputable. Perhaps treatment is now a bit more humane than the days when patients were chained and had little more than garbage to eat in the state hospitals, yet the attitudes of many professionals who are supposed to be helping and understanding these people has not changed significantly in the last five decades.

There is one place in this world that demonstrates mental health disparity does not have to exist. This place is Geel, Belgium. For over 700 years this town with only a population of around 35,000 people, has shown love and concern for people who are mentally ill. Geel is known for its pioneering method of treating psychiatric patients. These patients receive treatment at the large hospital in town, but live in the community with families who host them. Living in the community these patients are able to take part in everyday life. They work alongside the townspeople, they eat with them, and they stay with the townspeople in their homes. This type living and working situation presents more opportunity for community integration and social interaction. Thus the patients in Geel have a better chance of living more meaningful lives. It also means they have a better chance of recovering from their mental health diagnosis. The citizens of Geel have opened their doors since 1249 to people living with mental illness. This community model is perhaps the oldest known recovery model of mental health care. Successful recovery allows people with mental health problems greater ability to function as responsible members of the community. Thus, it's logical to encourage a concept of "community recovery" in which communities live with, rather than fear, people with mental illness. The mental patients in Geel are often "adopted" by the host families for life. If a patient has to return to the hospital for a stay, the town holds a meeting to determine what mistakes might have been made to cause this. The town feels it is the town who has failed the mental patient in this case, rather than the mental patient failing the system. This is truly a mental health system with no disparities.

Change without Changing

The treatment of people with mental illness has changed a little, but in many respects still remains the same. People with a mental diagnosis are still regarded as sub-standard and needing to be "fixed." Mental health professionals often find themselves in the role of parents who never let their children mature. People with mental problems are segregated into group homes and apartments set outside for the mentally ill. Most of the group homes that I've been acquainted with over the years are not conducive to a person ever regaining any semblance of individuality. They are also not beneficial for a person's recovery. Group homes act as if their customers are children and they need to be the guardian. This is most likely caused by greed. If a person does get better, he or she would move and the group home would lose business. One group home I am familiar with charges $1200.00 per month. Unfortunately, the people who are in need of this type accommodation are on some type of disability from the government and cannot afford to pay that much money.

The apartments that I have seen also are not very helpful in regard to assisting a person in learning to live an independent life full of meaning and purpose. Here again, the people who run these type facilities act more as guardians making sure the residents take their medications, telling them they have to attend a day treatment program and generally teaching their residents to be more dependent upon the mental health system.

Residents' money is also controlled by these living situations. Often the person's entire disability check will be used to pay for rent and other necessities with the patient only receiving a small weekly allowance. In some cases, the patient receives no money from his check at all. This allowance is usually for the person to buy cigarettes and items like toilet tissue or other personal need items. If the person is living in an apartment facility, he is also given a very small amount of money; some are given $25.00 to buy groceries that must last an entire week. Thus, the person has freedom without really being free. I can understand the reasoning behind these living situations. They exist because mental health systems still believe the mentally ill incapable of making decisions. The mental patient, although an adult, is treated as if he or she were a child. Consequently, the more this happens the more dependence takes place on the part of the patient in regards to the mental health system. Years pass and no real progress is made by the patient because the patient is told indirectly he or she cannot make decisions. This makes people learn to not trust their abilities.

When a person learns not to trust his or her abilities, the person then becomes trapped in the mental health system. Mental health systems rely on this type thinking, thus, the mentally ill patient continues to go for years, even a lifetime, without growing into a productive citizen.

The bondage of people with mental illness is not that of chains now. It is bondage of mind. It is control. It is a demand for compliance to the mental health system, to the medications, and to compliance with the "treatment plan" that mental health professionals compose for the mentally ill. I might add this "treatment plan" is also a plan that seldom includes the patient's desires, the patient's goals or the patient's input.

People with mental illness are already filled with self-doubt, a lack of self-esteem, and lack of self-confidence. They are often served by a mental health system that contributes to these factors and feeds the idea to these people that they need to be "helped." Granted that some individuals may think they are in need of help, but this thinking is because the idea of recovery and regaining one's life is seldom taught. Indeed, the idea of maintenance – staying on medication, staying out of the hospital – is the emphasis. The question must then be posed: How does one stay out of the hospital if not taught the necessary skills to do this?

People with a mental health diagnosis have a need to learn to cope with life despite having a mental illness. However, rather than being taught the necessary skills to break free of dependence on the system, the mental patient often finds himself being taught to rely more heavily on the system and on medication that only soothes symptoms and rarely produces a cure.

The only real answers to life's problems come from within a person. The mental health patient is seldom made aware that he or she must strive toward solving life's problems. Nor is the mental patient taught there are some things one can do for one's self. Dependence upon the system is perpetually taught and the mental patient learns this one lesson extremely well.

Children learn from their parents; conversely, parents are often taught valuable lessons by their children. Children often teach parents the valuable lesson of looking at life in a simpler way. A child will pick a flower for his mother who has forgotten how wonderful it is to take the time to smell a rose. This gesture will remind the mother she should perhaps learn to appreciate life again. The child will bring his father a problem from school and together they will solve it. This teaches the father that life's problems should be examined in a less complex way.

However, mental health systems who think of themselves as guardians over their "children" have not yet begun to learn the valuable lessons their children are trying to teach them. When a mental patient tells his "parent" that he is uncomfortable doing something the system is trying to force upon him, the system often thinks of the patient as being non-compliant or as being a trouble-maker. If the patient gets too upset with the system, the patient will more than likely find himself forcefully admitted into a mental hospital on the pretext that he is being harmful to himself.

People were once brought to mental institutions for mundane reasons. A husband might be upset with a wife and have her committed to an institution because "she's acting strange." A parent would have a child placed in an institution because the child was unruly. Now, if a person is not considered harmful to himself or others, chances are the person will not be admitted. No longer can people be forced into a mental institution for years with no hope of ever being set free. The admission requirements have gotten more stringent in recent years because mental institutions were overcrowded and many of the patients were not severely mentally ill. Perhaps the admission requirements are tougher now but this is still change without changing.

It is change without changing in the sense that, although admittance into a mental hospital is tougher, the idea is still in existence that people should be admitted if they act strange or different from the norms of society. Society does not accept difference and individuality nor does it encourage independent thinking. Thus, a person who is different is considered strange and bizarre. Strange behavior is considered unacceptable and, to protect itself, society has historically imposed forced institutionalization upon those members whose behavior it deems bizarre. This idea has not changed a lot. People who act differently are still thought to be a risk to society. Society still segregates these people with placement in an institution by managing to prove they are potentially harmful to themselves or others around them.

The Hospital

So… you want to get well? Perhaps you've gotten to the point you are thinking of going to a mental hospital. This may seem the logical thing for you to do to get better. It may be your only option if you have reached a point you feel you can no longer handle the stressors of life and you are thinking of doing harm to yourself or someone else. However, please be aware there are ways you can prevent this from happening. These ways are discussed in my book <u>Beyond Psychology: Learning to Live a Life of Your Own.</u> The next few pages will describe what happens when you go into a mental hospital. Please note that if you have insurance and can afford a private hospital the following description might not be relevant to you. The description that follows will be more relevant to people admitted into a state run facility.

Admission: The process involved during admission is the same whether admitted into a private hospital or a state facility. If your behavior is considered strange or threatening, you will have more than one police officer who will approach you. Within a few moments of this approach, you will find yourself in handcuffs and, possibly, in leg or ankle chains. This is standard operating procedure with almost every police department. The words "mental patient" is often equated with violence. This is promulgated by the news and television media. However, there is no more violence among the mentally ill than among the general population in this country.

After your encounter with the police, you will be taken to a local emergency room before you will be taken to a mental hospital. People with mental illness generally have long waits at emergency rooms. You are taken to an emergency room first because you can't be admitted into a mental hospital until you have been cleared medically. I have known people who have had to wait 16 – 24 hours, or longer, in emergency rooms until a bed can become available at a mental hospital.

When you finally reach a mental hospital be prepared to forget your former life. Again you may be transported by police officers who will again place you in handcuffs. Even if you are taken to a mental hospital in an ambulance, you will be restrained in some manner until you reach the hospital.

During the admission process at the mental hospital, you will have a cursory examination to make sure your blood pressure and glucose levels are within range. You will also be scanned to make sure you have no metal objects on your person. If you have a belt on your pants, this will be taken from you and placed with all your other personal belongings until you are discharged. If you have brought cigarettes, a lighter, a wallet, a purse, money, deodorant, shoe laces – any type of personal item – these will be taken from you as well.

Your Stay at the hospital: During your time spent in a mental hospital forget any ideas of personal freedom. This is not an ordinary hospital. If you have been admitted and identified as potentially harmful to yourself, you will be watched for 24 hours. This means someone will be assigned to watch your every move to make sure you do not harm yourself. If you "behave" during this time, you will be promoted to a different level of care and won't have someone shadowing you. Once you are on a different level of care you will still be watched, but from a distance. A worker in the hospital unit where you are assigned will document your location every 15 minutes until you are discharged.

Further, you will not have a lot to do during your stay. Television is turned off during the day time while you receive treatment. This treatment consists of a doctor seeing you, a case manager talking with you, and the mandatory attendance of group sessions during the day. The rest of the day you must spend socializing with other patients. Most mental hospitals do not allow the patient to return to his or her room until bed time. This is accomplished by locking the patient's room during the daylight hours. From the time the patient arrives at the mental hospital until the patient is discharged there is a prevalence of boredom.

Privacy is almost nil in mental hospitals. For example, if a male wants to shave, there must be a staff member present with him in the restroom. Many shower areas have no curtains so there is no privacy. Ladies

21

restroom areas are the same. Many times there are not enough workers in mental hospitals to ensure the safety of males or females during these times.

No, a mental hospital is not home. If you get thirsty or hungry at home you can eat or drink. In a mental hospital water is available when you wish it, but forget about having tea or cola when you want it. Food is available during lunch and snack time and sometimes these times do not follow the prescribed schedule. If the unit you are placed on is understaffed, your meals may be a little late. If another patient is acting out, the chances of your meal not being on time also increases until that patient has settled down and the unit returns to normal.

You are awakened early in the morning. Although you are an adult, staff in the hospital is going to ask you if you have had a bowel movement in the last 24 hours. They do this because the medication you are taking can cause constipation. They also do this because people have died from not having a bowel movement in state hospitals. As a result of these deaths, patients are now given a laxative to prevent this. You may not need the laxative, but if staff feels you should have it, you will take it. Of course eating foods that are healthy will prevent this also. Also, early in the morning you are going to be asked if you have bathed. If you have not bathed and possess some type of body odor, you may be harassed into taking a bath.

You will also spend a lot of time reflecting on your life while you are in hospital. Many hospitals do not have activity therapists. This means arts, craft work, music and any activities have almost ceased to exist. State hospital budgets have been cut so deeply that most hospitals can only afford "essential" personnel. So time passes slowly because there is no activity happening. Funding for hospitals is one of the major disparities for people with mental illness. Without funding, hospitals cannot keep adequate personnel, much less make mental patients comfortable and feed them properly.

Your safety is another factor you need to consider while a patient in a state institution. While working in two state mental hospitals in Georgia, the author has witnessed almost daily violence among patients and staff.

Mental patients are less likely to be violent when among the community setting than when placed in an institution. Those who are hospitalized tend to be more violent because their symptoms are much more present and acute. The strict admission policies to a mental hospital that are in place now are partly the cause of this. As stated earlier in this book, for a person to be admitted to a state hospital the person must be considered a danger to self or to others. Since this is the case, violence in state hospitals is more prevalent than ever before. This fact coupled with understaffing has made mental hospitals unsafe.

While you are in a mental hospital a case manager will present you with a treatment plan. This treatment plan will consist of the goals that you need to accomplish. It is actually a plan that the case manager is supposed to do with your input. You are the one who is supposed to tell the case manager your goals and the interventions needed to help you achieve those goals. This does not always happen. Case managers often take it upon themselves to do this without your input. This is often a mistake. Sometimes the case managers will set goals for you to accomplish that you are not interested in accomplishing. If you have not set your own goals, the likelihood of you wanting to achieve the goals set for you is small. However, if you want to be discharged from the hospital, you must make an effort to accomplish the goals whether you like them or not. This is unfairness toward the mental patient that has been addressed in the past, but which still takes place. This is another example of "change without changing."

Discharge from the hospital: When you have met certain requirements you will be discharged from the hospital. Most mental hospitals must be assured that you will have a safe place to live when you are discharged. If you are homeless this will mean you will stay in the hospital until accommodations can be arranged for you. These accommodations are usually a group home setting. At one time mental hospitals in Georgia would discharge patients to a homeless shelter. When this happened the patient would often end up again on the streets and be back in another hospital within a few days.

You must also meet the requirement that you are stable enough to be discharged from the hospital. If you are stable you must agree to continue to take the medication your doctor will prescribe. Many hospitals now provide patients with a 5 – 7 day supply of medication. Patients are then told they must see a psychiatrist within 5 – 7 days to obtain another prescription for these medications. Mental health systems with contracts from the state *must* see the patient within that time frame. However, sometimes patients are missed because they do not appear at the appointment the hospital made for them with the mental health provider. Patients will then deplete their medication and often find themselves back in the hospital within a few days.

Many times patients are discharged too soon. A large number of mental hospitals have a goal of discharging the patient within 7 days if possible. This goal of 7 days is sometimes a little too quick because the patient has not stabilized completely. Many patients discharged too quickly find themselves without the necessary coping skills to face everyday stressors and must again face being hospitalized.

Perhaps the biggest challenge a mental health patient faces during the whole process of admission, stay, and discharge from the mental hospital is that of losing control of his or her life. The mental patient, already experiencing loss of friends, family, and even the possibility of loss of job, will find himself faced with a loss of freedom. He or she will no longer be in total control of life.

I work in a mental hospital. A patient once told me that the last decision he had made was two hours prior to his hospitalization. "Since then," he stated, "the hospital has made all my decisions for me." During the hospital process the mental patient is told what to do, when to get up, when to go to bed, when to eat, when to attend group sessions, and has little or no choice in the process. This treatment is likened to the old days when mental patients were chained to walls. This is still "change without changing."

The Mental Health Clinic

Once you are discharged from the state hospital you will be referred to a mental health clinic for further treatment. Your first appointment with the mental health clinic will be made by your case manager at the hospital. You must appear for this appointment. This is necessary because the doctor you will be seeing will examine you for your further need of medication. This visit will last you approximately 15 – 30 minutes. Subsequent visits to your doctor will last only around 15 minutes if you are lucky. Until he knows you, your doctor will prescribe medication for 30 days at a time. Initially you will need to see him once a month. Once the doctor feels he can trust you to take your medication as prescribed he will schedule you to see him every three months. When this happens, your medication can be refilled every month for that three month period.

If your doctor feels you need to see someone more frequently, you will be scheduled to see a counselor on a regular basis. You may see a counselor once a week or once a month for perhaps 30 minutes per session. During this session, the counselor will encourage you to discuss the matters that are troubling you. Your doctor may also recommend you attend some type of program during the day depending upon how serious your condition presents to him.

This description of mental health clinics sounds somewhat banal or commonplace. However, the truth about mental health centers is far different from the brief description the author has given you.

The truth about mental health centers is there is a preponderance of emphasis placed upon medication and medication compliance. As a result, mental health patients, their doctors, and their counselors have come to rely too much on chemicals to solve problems. While it may be true the medications replace the chemicals within the brain that may not be present, these chemicals also do not produce a lasting effect and they most certainly do not produce a cure for mental illness. The only benefit a person receives from psychotropic medications is that of helping the person remain stable – that is, as long as the person takes the medication. If the mental health patient believes strongly the medication is helping, then the medication is the predominant factor for stability. This factor alone accounts for billions of dollars spent each year for mental health medication. People have come to believe if they have a problem that taking another pill will solve that problem.

Another dilemma with mental health centers is that they are not actually teaching the skills the mentally ill person needs to be able to live a fuller, more meaningful life. True, the counselors and doctors listen to you the few minutes you are in their presence, yet it is you who must go home and live within your skin, endure your trials, and meet the challenges of your life. No doctor, no counselor, no pill can solve your problem. The medication makes the problem seem more bearable, the counselor helps you by listening and the doctor diagnoses and prescribes, but when you are alone in your home, the person in you is the one who must finally decide how you are going to overcome the challenges you are facing. If you are not prepared to face these challenges you will not grow beyond them. At some point during your mental illness you will need to learn the skills that will help you overcome this illness. You will not learn these skills at a mental health center, especially if that mental health center is operating under the medical model of mental health care rather than the recovery model. The medical model seeks to alleviate symptoms, prescribes medications and involves the patient in therapy while the recovery model assists the patient in learning the skills to stay well and to find meaning and purpose in life that can eventually guide the patient to become employed again. The recovery model also teaches the patient how to use the resources that are available in the community to assist in staying well once discharged from the hospital. While the medical model treats the mind, the recovery model treats the whole person and realizes the patient is more than a diagnosis.

Faceless

If you have experienced mental illness in any of its treacherous forms you may have looked in a mirror one morning and wondered who the person in the mirror was that was looking back at you. You did not recognize yourself. Your mind told you that this was not the face that you grew to know while becoming an adult. You felt as though you were staring at the face of a stranger and that stranger looked only vaguely familiar to you. However, you at least saw a face and were aware that it was your face no matter how strange it looked to you. Your counselor and your doctor may not see a face at all. They will see a diagnosis. That is their jobs.

Most psychiatrists are not seeing you as a person. Instead they listen to your symptoms as you talk with them. They listen, they nod their heads, and they prescribe medication. When it comes to you they do not see a face. They do not see an individual. They see symptoms. They see sickness. They do not understand that you are a whole person and that sometimes it is better to treat that whole person and not just that person's symptoms.

Although psychiatrists and mental health professionals see you as faceless, society views you with having a face of ugliness and doesn't see beyond your behavior to understand. You are violent to them. Your strange behavior isn't acceptable. You are then ostracized, cast out, separated and deemed as a threat to society's "normalcy." Remember that the psychiatrists and mental health professionals from whom you seek assistance also come from this same society.

As a result, you look into your bathroom mirror in the morning and you see yourself as faceless. You do not see the beauty within you because you are listening to those around you who see only your illness and the behavior which is a result of your illness. You see the ugliness that others see. Sometimes, because you see no face and only see ugliness, you may find yourself behaving in the bizarre ways of your mental illness.

When you have become faceless to yourself then you are not you. You become that faceless, ugly individual that you think others around you see. You have then lost identity. The disparity you have encountered from the mental health system has then turned into despair. This despair, coupled with the mental health problem you already have, makes your desire to do anything decrease. This lack of desire to do anything will cause you to cease being an individual whose life is full of meaning and purpose.

Mental Health Programs

If you have a severe and persistent mental health problem, chances are you will be referred to some type of mental health program. These programs vary in intensity and length of treatment. Generally, you may be recommended to attend or be a part of this program for at least one year. During this year you will be expected to participate regularly either by attending or being involved.

Assertive Community Treatment (ACT): This program is designed to serve people in their homes. The original intention was to assist people with severe mental problems to remain stable, to gain insight into their problems, and to eventually take control of their lives. It was also designed to assist people in learning the skills needed to stay out of the hospital. Originally, the main emphasis of ACT was for an interdisciplinary team to meet with the individual 3 or more times per week to encourage and teach independent living skills to the patient. Its primary function was to do whatever was necessary to help keep the person out of the hospital.

This author has experience working with two ACT teams. So the information you are receiving is not second hand information, but is derived from the author's lived experience. From the observations made while working with ACT, I would not advise anyone with mental health problems who can think half-way clearly to be part of this program. As it was executed where I worked, the ACT program does not teach independence. It has evolved into primarily a transportation program. Participants are transported to doctor's appointments, grocery stores, and to fast food restaurants. They are taken shopping at Wal- Mart, Goodwill, and other stores, rather than being taught how to use the community resources available for transportation. While they are at these places of business, the recipients of ACT services are not being taught to shop wisely. Rather than being instructed about calorie and carbohydrate content of food, rather than being shown how to recognize the best buy for their money, the recipients of ACT are often left to buy primarily what they want to buy. ACT was never

36

intended to be an instrument to rule over people, but was intended to teach independence and how to use the community resources available to its recipients so those recipients could live a full life, independently, in the communities of their choice.

It has become a program that is little more than a state hospital in that it tells its patients what to do and when it can be done. It teaches dependence and encourages the participant to rely more on the program than on the participant's decision making ability. More emphasis is made on the person taking medication than on teaching the person the independent living skills necessary to create a life beyond the mental health system. ACT programs cause participants to feel that if it wasn't for ACT, they would not be able to do anything. Here, again, is the idea that the mentally ill person is incapable of making decisions. I once worked with an ACT program that took a person's vehicle from her because the lady had been found in a parking lot at a local business confused and dazed. The point is that it doesn't matter if the person was confused and dazed or even if the lady had been found in her vehicle doing some bizarre behavior like masturbating in public, her vehicle should not have been confiscated. Mental patients still have the right to own property and to vote among many other rights that seem to have been forgotten. If she wished I am positive this person would have a good case in court. However, she has been so brow beaten by the mental health system she is afraid that other rights might be taken from her.

Further, if people who participate with ACT do not follow the medication regimen and treatment plan that has been recommended for them, there is a likelihood they could be taken to mental health court and a judge issue a court order to make the person take medication and follow the treatment plan. If the person does not comply with the court order, that person will spend some time in jail. How is this teaching a person that it is possible to regain his or her life and become a contributing citizen to the community? It does not.

Psychosocial Rehabilitation (PSR): A person who attends a PSR program typically is in the program 4 – 6 hours per day for five days a week. These programs are attended by individuals the mental health system has deemed as not functioning well. While engaged in the program the people learn basic hygiene, coping skills, anger management, and social skills. They are individuals whom the mental health system feels need something to do during the day to occupy their time. Many states think of these programs more as adult day care programs or adult babysitting programs. Marvelous in its concept, the PSR program could be a great program if it wasn't for the idea that the people who attend are considered "lower functioning adults." This concept alone tells the people who attend these programs that they are different from main stream society. One would think that the word "rehabilitation" included in the title of these programs would mean that the person is there to regain life and become independent again. This, however, is not the reality of the program.

In actuality, the program has evolved into a place for people to attend to become tremendously bored. You would be bored, too, if you knew that every Tuesday you were going to be taught again how to brush your teeth or wash your hands properly. In fact you would be absolutely angry because you may have been told you **must** attend the program or the mental health system would withdraw its assistance to you. Often the treatment plan in which you were not allowed to participate may state you must attend the program or remain in the state hospital. If you withdraw from the program before the system feels you are ready, you may be committed to the state hospital again.

Peer Support: A peer support program is also usually a 4 - 6 hour program for people with mental illness. Peer Support programs usually have people whose functioning level is considered higher than those involved in PSR programs. The individuals who attend peer support are able to take care of hygiene and other basic needs without prompting. Peer support programs are designed to assist individuals in moving closer to becoming valuable citizens to the community in which they live. People enrolled in these programs are supposed to be taught about recovery from mental illness and how to

So... You Want to Get Well?

maintain their mental and physical health so they can eventually become responsible individuals again who can also become employable. The author has nothing negative to say about these programs as long as they are managed by capable people who demonstrate empathy with the participants who attend.

However, these programs, like PSR programs, are often looked upon by some people as having its chief purpose of being an adult daycare center. Like the PSR programs, some people think Peer Support should be a place for people to come so they can be guarded during the time they spend at the program. Yet, if those who look upon Peer Support disdainfully would have a conversation with those who attend Peer Support, they would be told by the attendees how much this program actually helps them other than having a place to come to pass the time.

Intensive Case Management: In recent years this program has gained some popularity from the mental health system. However, it is only popular from the viewpoint of states who administer this program – not by

41

the people who are being forced to participate in them. This program is not intended to assist people with a mental problem, but to manage them and to rule over them. There is little human contact with patients from those who work in these programs. Most contact is through telephone calls and only occasional visitation. Mostly, staff who work these programs want to make sure the patient is compliant with his or her medication regimen. Little or no skills are taught and the patient generally shows no improvement. This program is another waste of tax payer money because it does little good in improving the life of the patient. With this program, if the patient does not comply with what staff feels he or she should do, the patient can end up court ordered back into a mental institution. This is blatant coercion by staff and this program needs to be defunded in all states.

There are, of course, more mental health programs than those discussed in these pages. However, the ones discussed are the ones in which the author has experience. The author is aware that there are ACT programs who actually live up to the ACT model and who have people graduate from the program to live satisfying, meaningful lives. A mental health program needs to be a program that helps the participant grow and eventually demonstrate no further need for the program. It should not be a program that teaches further dependence on the mental health system.

The Dilemma

If you happen to be mentally ill in the United States, you will most likely receive treatment in programs that are underfunded, from people who are not paid well, and those two factors can become a dilemma for you, the patient. Underfunded programs mean that the quality of care you receive may not be the best you deserve. It also may mean – especially if you are in a state hospital – that your safety may be compromised. Having too few staff on duty also means you may not receive adequate treatment. This, in turn, will mean a longer hospital stay. Similarly, if you are involved in treatment with some type of mental health program, the lack of proper funding for that program may mean that the staff serving you may not have the credentialing that better paid programs would have. This means that the training they have received is not always suitable or conducive to your recovery.

Inadequately trained and underpaid staff are not

always sympathetic toward those with mental problems. I have witnessed staff that is rude to clients/patients. I have also known staff that are overworked who have made derogatory statements to those people they are supposed to be helping. There is no excuse for mistreatment of patients/clients, but be aware that this can sometimes happen if you are involved in a program or incarcerated in a hospital. I say "incarcerated" because people who are in a hospital are often there against their will.

These factors have come under the scrutiny of the Department of Justice in recent years. In the State of Georgia, a series of articles which appeared in the Atlanta Journal-Constitution prompted an investigation into Georgia's mental health system and its mental hospitals. Some of Georgia's mental hospitals have now been closed as a result of this investigation. Georgia denies the closings were a result of the federal investigation and cites financial reasons for these closings. At the same time, Georgia wants to spend six to eleven million dollars opening up a state of the art central mental health facility (hospital) which would serve the entire state. Their reasoning is that there are only 300 – 400 people who need hospitalization on any given day and that having more than one hospital is a waste of resources. Georgia further reasons that the money spent to run more than one state hospital would be better spent in opening more community services. This is reasonable thinking, but three state hospitals have been closed and, so far, no improvement in community services has taken place. In fact, since the hospital closing in Rome, Georgia, that city has been doing everything it can to get the mental hospital reopened because the closing has overburdened the community. People now have to go without the treatment they need and deserve. The number of homeless people who are mentally ill has also increased as a result of that hospital closing. Some patients are now being transported hundreds of miles to a hospital and, when discharged, are often assigned to programs that are not in their original home communities. The more severe cases are assigned to group homes in the city where the hospital is located and may never see their homes again.

To open a new, large centralized hospital is reminiscent of what Georgia had 50 years ago. At that time there was only one state hospital. People would have to travel far away from their home towns to be served by this hospital. This hospital was known as Milledgeville State Hospital. It later became known as Central State Hospital. It no longer serves as a mental hospital, but is open only to serve the criminally insane. In the 1960's, this hospital had over 13,000 patients who were mentally ill. Having a central hospital again would be detrimental to mental health patients. Although Georgia states there are only 300 to 400 people mentally ill on any given day, I suspect the number is much higher than this and, based on the experience with Central State Hospital, a central hospital would soon be overcrowded. Having a central hospital again would mean that patients would once more have to be hospitalized hundreds of miles from home. It would also mean that patients would again become meaningless numbers to the State of Georgia and to the personnel hired to work in that hospital. It would further indicate that Georgia would be going backward in time and repeating the same mistakes it made with Central State Hospital. Moreover, a reversal to a large centralized hospital would mean that an already confused and lost patient would become just another cog in the wheel of the mental health machine of Georgia. Disparity for the mental patient served in this atmosphere would soon turn into despair. People would be forgotten as they were 50 years ago and would soon be lost to ever having a chance at "normalcy."

Dr. Jeffery Schaler, in his article, *Strategies of Psychiatric Coercion,* (Published in Cato Unbound, A Journal of Debate, 8/6/2012) stated, "While from my perspective I would oppose the violation of even one person's rights through psychiatric coercion – while I would oppose even one person being involuntarily committed to a prison called a mental hospital – in reality thousands of people are held in mental institutions across the United States at any given time. Some were forced into a psychiatric facility and cannot get out. Others chose to enter a facility voluntarily and can't get out. A large part of treating mental illness involves forced medication and forced electroshock therapy (ECT)...

"Most people recognize that literal treatment for literal disease is a choice, subject to consent. People have the right to refuse treatment when they have lung cancer, or are otherwise very sick, despite the fact that doing so may mean certain death. When you elect to undergo major surgery, you must sign a consent form. Even when you request a vaccination for influenza, you still must sign a consent form. There are three relatively uncontroversial situations in which treatment proceeds legally without consent: The first is the medical treatment of children. The second is the treatment of people when they are literally unconscious. And the third is the treatment of persons with contagious disease... Most people accept these three situations or conditions as legal and ethically sound... Psychiatrists, on the other hand, twist these rather uncontroversial cases in extremely self-serving ways. They do this despite the fact that they tell us over and over again that mental diseases are just like physical diseases and that mental patients should be treated exactly as people with real, physical diseases are treated."

Dr. Schaler further states in his article: "Treatment without consent for "mental illness" is justified by saying the person is like a child. Since we base the distinction between adult and child on chronological age, a person is either an adult or a child. If he's twenty-one, he's an adult. If he's twenty, he's a child. Psychiatrists and mental health professionals empowered by the state to commit someone involuntarily to a psychiatric "hospital" argue that a twenty-five year old person who refuses to bathe and take care of himself is really a child. He does not, in their opinion, exercise responsibility for himself because he cannot do so. He is a threat to himself. He may verbally or nonverbally abdicate all responsibility for himself and ask to be taken care of by others, for fear that he might hurt himself. (Again, I am most concerned with those who do not want help, who reject "help," and who are coerced into "treatment" when they don't want it.)

"It doesn't matter to me whether they express a "thank you clause" after they are released from a hospital, or after they are thoroughly drugged with major tranquilizers. In my opinion, when an adult refuses treatment his refusal must be respected. Otherwise, coercion occurs in the name of helping him. The intentions of psychiatrists and this man's friends and family are irrelevant. They may certainly try to persuade, encourage, and even beg him to go into a "treatment" facility. In the end, the man called a child has a right to refuse treatment and that refusal must be respected in the sense that psychiatrists keep their hands off him."

Thus, part of the dilemma you may face - aside from poor funding, inadequate personnel, and hospitalization - may be that of coercion from mental health professionals. As I have stated earlier in this work, people with mental illness are still regarded as children. They are treated as children and regarded as being incapable of making their own decisions. The consensus of thinking is children must be made to do things for their own good. Hence, a mentally ill adult person, considered a child, must be coerced, forced, into treatment or hospitalization.

Perhaps the strongest statement Dr. Schaler, the

renowned psychiatrist, wrote in his article is the following:

"The greatest medical legal fiction since the Civil War is mental illness, the idea that persons labeled as mentally ill are not full persons, full citizens, entitled to their full constitutional rights. It is as if the Bill of Rights had a postscript at the bottom reading "For mentally healthy people only.""

Part Two:

Maneuvering Through the Maze

of Mental Illness

Finding Your Way

In my book, <u>Beyond Psychology: Learning to Live a Life of Your Own,</u> I gave the reader several exercises to assist in maintaining mental health. You no doubt have a desire to feel better and do better or you would not be reading this book. Yet, if you really do want to feel better and do well in life, you must find your way despite the disparities in mental health treatment. Right now you may be asking yourself "How do I do this?" Hopefully, by the time you have finished reading this book, you will have some knowledge of methods to find your way through the darkness of mental illness and the disparities of mental health treatment. If you do not have a mental health diagnosis, perhaps this work will give you some insight into dealing with a loved one who does have a mental problem.

People with mental problems are unique individuals who often think of themselves with distaste. Often these individuals have low self-esteem, exhibit behavior that sometimes is not quite accepted by the general population, and are stigmatized by those who supposedly love them. Negative actions toward people with mental problems exacerbate their symptoms making them more withdrawn and isolative. Sometimes they are not easy to live with because their symptoms come into play and their behavior will strike those close to them as odd. This behavior is sometimes considered unacceptable, but it is still their behavior. The reality of a person with a mental health diagnosis is still reality to that person, even as you or I know our own realities. When we do not accept people with these problems, we become part of the disparity in the treatment of the mentally ill. We expect people to accept us despite our faults, but often the acceptance of people with mental problems is low.

So... you, as a mental patient, want to get well? Of course you do. Since you want to get well let's explore what wellness is and discuss how you can achieve wellness yourself. Please note that this discussion involves your mental wellness as well as other aspects of wellness. Why? Because you are a whole person – not just a mental illness.

Wellness, described, is an overall feeling of pleasantness. When you feel good you are able to accomplish the things you set out to do. When you are well, you are not overwhelmed by your symptoms and you don't feel like a stranger to yourself. You are able to face friends and family and not let the things they may say or do affect how you feel. Being well has many aspects. When you are well, your emotional, physical, and spiritual aspects are in harmony with each other. Also, you understand your relationships with other people. You can learn quicker and apply what you learn to your life. Wellness, then, is the state of being healthy in body, mind and spirit. Each of these aspects can have an effect upon the other. If you are not well in body, this can make you feel ill in the other two aspects as well. If you are emotionally unwell, your body and spirit can be affected. To achieve whole body wellness, one must realize these three aspects come into play and work on keeping them in harmony with each other.

Finding your way through the maze of mental illness into the journey called recovery is a difficult task, but one that can be done. Getting outside that maze without becoming terribly lost is more difficult. You will find that people around you will be discouraging and try to tell you recovery from mental illness is not possible. However, recovery is happening every day to people who believe it, who live it, and who have gained their lives back after their nightmare of mental illness. What is seemingly impossible is overcoming the stigma that exists because you have had a mental illness. The worse thing to overcome is living with the inequities in the mental health system while you have a mental problem.

There is not a perfect solution to your mental health problem. Medication will help, learning the skills you need to survive mental illness will help, finding your way through the maze will help, but, in the end, it is you who must decide to help yourself. It is you who must learn what you need to do to get well and to stay well. It is you who must *work* on your problems. You must have the resolve to do all this and to endure the hardships you will face while you are finding your way through the maze of mental illness and mental health inequities.

Method in the Madness

According to the National Alliance on Mental Illness about 57 million Americans will be affected by some type of mental health problems this year. This is equal to one in four people facing an upsetting time in their lives. About one in seventeen people will be affected by a serious mental illness that will cause their lives to be changed drastically. The same statistics also state that for 70 to 90 percent of those affected by mental illness, the chance for recovery is significant. Those people who do find it through the maze of mental illness will have worked hard to achieve wellness again. They will be the people who are willing to engage in their own healing process with a positive attitude. They will also have learned some method in their madness to be able to achieve this wellness.

Those people who do find their way through the maze will also have become their own best friend. They will have learned to resist self-deprecation and self-defeat. They will have learned that within themselves they have the power to overcome the devastation they are experiencing. How will they do this? They will have learned some of the methods I am about to give in this chapter.

Dr. Marie Hartwell-Walker wrote in an article: "Becoming Your Own Best Friend" (*Psych Central Magazine)* to get real. If you think there is a "cure" for severe and persistent mental illness, you are setting yourself up for a big disappointment. If you are your own best friend, you would be like any other good friend who would remind you that people with hypertension or arthritis cannot be totally cured, but they can live happy productive lives despite the symptoms. Even mentally ill people can experience a better quality of life despite their diagnosis by engaging in a healthy lifestyle.

If you are your own best friend you will know that taking your medication is important also. Although medication is not a cure for mental illness, it will generally assist you in being able to think more clearly.

The author's ideas of medication are that it is better to take the medication than to constantly be in and out of a mental hospital because you have not yet learned to control your symptoms without it. Pills alone will not keep you well. You will need to find someone you can trust that you can talk with as well.

Part of staying mentally well is getting enough rest. This means you might need to establish some regular time in which you try to go to sleep. Overstimulation during evening hours will make sleep more difficult so you would need to try to slow things way down in the early evening. Another method to help you rest is watching your intake of caffeine during the evening. Sugar intake should also be decreased in the early evening as well. Carbohydrates will cause you to have energy and having that energy will keep you from sleeping well. Turn off any television program that may cause too much excitement also. Take a warm soothing bath, play some soft music, and slow your thinking down. Establish a similar routine each night to accustom your body to being able to relax when it's time for bed.

If you are your own best friend you would learn relaxation exercises. A good friend would help you learn to meditate and encourage you to learn the relaxation response or yoga – anything that would help you learn to relax. Prayer helps some people. You are the master of your body. You would know if your mind is racing and that you need to slow it down.

If you are your own best friend you will know that having more friends is important. People who are isolated have a much more difficult time managing their illness. As your own best friend, you would recognize the need for social contacts in your life. You make social contacts by being involved in church or some type of support group. Avoid the bar scene because you will leave feeling more lonely than when you went inside. You may also feel more depressed because you may realize no true friends have been formed within that environment.

Many people think that being mentally healthy means you never experience bad times or emotional problems. We all go through disappointments, loss, and change. These are a "normal" part of life. However, if a person is not mentally healthy, it is very difficult for that person to adapt to adversity, hardship, and the changes which life brings. Experiencing this difficulty will bring depression; not knowing how to handle this difficulty causes symptoms to worsen. People who have good mental health are able to "bounce back" from adversity, overcome hardships and learn that life is all about change. This is a marvelous aspect of healing called resiliency.

One key factor in resiliency is having the ability to balance your stress and emotions. The ability to recognize your emotions and to express them in a healthy manner keeps you from getting stuck in a negative mood state like depression or anxiety. Another key factor of resiliency is having a strong support system. Having people you feel you can trust and who will encourage you will boost your resiliency when times are tough.

Emotional wellness refers to your overall psychological well-being. It includes how you feel about yourself, the quality of your relationships, and your ability to manage your feelings and the difficulties you face in life. Mental and emotional wellness refers to the presence of positive characteristics in a person. Some of those characteristics include:

- *Having a sense of contentment.* A person who is mentally healthy experiences more peace within himself than conflict.

- *Having a zest for life and for living.* The person actually enjoys being alive and lives life enthusiastically.

- *Knowing how to deal with stress.* A mentally healthy person does not allow the stressors he experiences to keep him down. He has the ability to "bounce back."

- *Has a sense of meaning and purpose in life.* Every individual needs to feel hope. Knowing you have a purpose in life brings hope.

- *Nurtures relationships with other people.* You encourage friendships and bring positive thoughts to those you call "friend."

- ***Learns new things and adapts to change.*** You know that life is about discovery and you can change your life.

- ***Can balance work and play; rest and activity.*** You realize the need to have equilibrium in your life. You do not let any aspect of your life outweigh the importance of the other aspects in your life.

- ***Has self-confidence and healthy self esteem.*** You are able to express confidence in yourself without coming across as conceited.

- ***Can recognize what is real and what is fantasy.*** You know the difference between reality and imagination.

- ***Enjoys Learning.***

These characteristics of emotional health allow a person to participate in life fully and help when a person is faced with the challenges and stresses of life.

To find some method in the madness it's important to pay attention to your own needs and feelings. If you let negative feelings build, they will cause your symptoms to worsen and make you sicker. Similarly, if you let stress get the better of you, you will find yourself less healthy emotionally and physically. Try to keep some kind of balance with the things you must do and the things that you really enjoy doing. Taking care of your own needs and feelings will help you be better prepared to face the challenges as they arise.

Taking care of your own needs and feelings will mean doing activities that release endorphins in your brain. Endorphins are chemicals that contribute to your overall feeling of being well. These chemicals are released in the brain in several ways:

1. Exercise.

2. Doing things that make others feel valued.

3. Practicing self-control.

4. Discovering the world around you.

5. The enjoyment of beauty in nature and art.

6. Limiting unhealthy mental habits like worry.

7. Taking care of a pet.

8. Enjoying leisure activities.

9. Meditation (prayer, yoga, relaxation exercises).

The important thing is that you realize you have strength within yourself you can learn to use to maintain your emotional wellness.

Most people think of being mentally health as being happy. This is not the case. People with good mental health will still have problems. There will be some days when the mentally healthy person will be sad, there will be some days of confusion about life and how to live it, and there will be days when even the most mentally healthy person may experience some self-doubt. However, the mentally healthy person knows that all these things are only temporary and in knowing this they can handle life much easier than a person who is experiencing symptoms of some mental disorder.

The mentally healthy person accepts the idea that bad things sometimes happen, but he or she does not allow these bad things to keep them locked in a state of despair.

The Family Perspective

Your family, friends, and other people who care about you are the ones who must come to an understanding of you and your illness. So this chapter is written for you and your family.

Your family member has been diagnosed with a mental illness. Do not become a part of the disparity of treatment that exists for those with a mental problem. Yes, your family member is acting a bit out of the ordinary. He or she may have said or done things to hurt you. I have met parents who refuse to see their child again because they are afraid of the child's mental illness. Your child, although he or she may not realize it, needs you now more than ever. You have always been there for your child before. You need to be there for that child now.

When your loved one is acting bizarre, you realize something needs to be done. However, there are some

69

signs that can tell you things are going wrong long before the loved one begins acting strangely.

If a loved one begins exhibiting any of the following signs, it is possible that the person is beginning to deteriorate and needs more understanding and assurance:

- *Inability to sleep at all or does not feel the need to sleep.* This is a common sign that exists with certain mental health disorders.

- *Feeling hopeless, down, helpless or needy.* The person is experiencing some loss of self-esteem in this early phase of mental illness.

- *Stating "I can't think like I used to."* When someone is experiencing symptoms of a mental problem, often the person may describe an inability to concentrate. If you will observe your loved one, you may notice this happening without being told.

- *Expressing negative thoughts, self-destructive thoughts, experiencing nightmares that upset.*

These can often be signs a person is beginning to experience some type of problem.

- *Using alcohol, illegal substances, increased tobacco use to cope with emotions.* These signs are extreme signs which do not occur in every person. However, should you notice them in your loved one, do not be judgmental. It would be better to be understanding and to gently begin suggesting the person seek professional help.

- *Inability to cope with the stressors of daily life.* If the person who could once handle the problems of everyday life begins to show anger or hostility, there is more than likely an inner problem happening that needs to be handled.

- *Suicidal Thoughts* If your loved one begins to express thoughts of self-harm "You'd be better off without me, I don't want to live" or thoughts similar to this, it may be time to go to a hospital.

As a person who cares, you naturally want to be helpful to your loved one who is experiencing mental problems. One of the best ways you can help is by realizing this is a _person_ you love who is ill. The person is not some monster or someone with a highly contagious disease. That person you love is still there, but the symptoms of the illness have changed the way that individual is acting. He or she will be trying at times, but the best thing you could do is understand. You must realize that most of the behavior the person is exhibiting cannot be helped. You need to also realize that the person may not realize how he is behaving because of the illness.

Some positive ways you can help your loved one during this time are as follows:

1. _Learn all you can_ about mental illness in general and about the diagnosis your loved one has been given specifically.

2. _Find practical ways to help._ Someone living with

mental illness may not always feel like cleaning the house. When you are ill with any type disease, a clean house may seem to be the least important thing in the world. You can help by offering to do this for the person.

3. *Listen and learn.* Sometimes all it takes to help someone is to be a good listener. A good listener lets the person express his thoughts without judging the person. When you listen, you can usually learn how a person is feeling and what the person needs from you to help him feel better.

4. *Know this too shall pass.* You may think this is an illness your loved one cannot get over, but the statistics indicate there is a huge percentage of likelihood the person will get better. Try to encourage your loved one by showing that you believe in him. This will inspire hope in the person.

5. *Encourage the person to make social contacts.* Isolating one's self from friends is a by-product of

mental illness. On the other hand, the person's friends need to also be encouraged to visit. Sometimes friends tend to withdraw from people with a mental health diagnosis.

6. *Encouragement in other aspects of life.* Your loved one will need to be encouraged gently in other ways. He may need to be reminded of his appointments with his doctor. He – or she – may also need to be reminded to take care of his grooming needs when the symptoms are really bad. At these times, gentle reminders without nagging are all that is needed. Remember, the person is also an adult and might get very upset with you if these reminders are not done in a respectful manner.

7. *Use good judgment when dealing with your loved one.* There are some things which can make a person's symptoms worse. Sometimes some of those triggers are the very people the person cares about. During this time of sickness do not approach the person with statements like "Come

on, you can snap out of this!" Also, telling the person "You can pull yourself up by your boot straps if you try" is not very helpful. The person already feels helpless enough and statements that would indicate that the person's mental illness is his fault aren't helpful and will cause resentment. It would be more beneficial to help the person realize he is going to live beyond this bad time and that *you* are going to be there to support and love.

One last thought for you as a family member is to not blame yourself for your loved one's mental health problems. There are many reasons a person's mental health can deteriorate. A person can be predisposed to having a mental problem through genetic inheritance. Other factors can bring about mental illness including some type of situational crisis that will upset the person, alcohol and substance abuse, some type of physical injury, and other causes. The chief cause of mental illness being recognized by the National Alliance for the Mentally

Ill (NAMI) is having a brain chemistry imbalance.

You could contribute to the person's mental health problems if you do not understand the person, but you are not the *cause* of the problem.

Let me urge you to practice patience and understanding when dealing with your loved one. It is often simply showing you understand that can point the person with a mental health problem in the direction of recovery and hope.

"I'm Lost..."

If you have had a mental health problem for any length of time, you are feeling somewhat lost in the maze of doctors, counselors, medications, and the attitude other people sometimes may have toward you. This is a normal reaction. In fact, many people with similar problems often feel lost trying to navigate the maze of mental health care. Mental health care is almost a misnomer when one considers how many people are misunderstood who have mental problems. It is also a misnomer because often those people who work within mental health do not seem to really care.

Being lost in the maze of mental illness is like trying to find your way without a map or a navigation system in in a city where you've never been. You travel looking for the building you want to find. You know it's there, but you just can't find the street where it's located. Then, when you find the street you need, it's often not easy to find the address of the building. The street may branch off without you're realizing it. You have to double back and find the street again. If you are trying to find your

77

way through a maze with no idea of how to escape, the same feelings apply. You are lost. You feel a little panic. Which way do you go? Where do you turn? Should I stop and ask for directions? What if I stop and ask, will I be attacked by some stranger?

The more you try to find your way through the maze of mental illness, the more you realize how lost you really are and the more frustrated you become. You need to stop and find a map at some point. The male population seems to not admit when they are lost and they do not want to stop and ask for help. In reality, though, there is nothing wrong with anyone asking for help. It demonstrates that you realize you are lost. Psychologists call this having insight. When you have insight into your problems you can then begin to solve them. Only when you realize you are lost will you begin to ask someone who can help you find your way. Don't ever be too proud or too shy to admit you need help when you realize something is wrong.

Knowing When Something is Wrong

You have been having something strange happening to you. You, perhaps, have no idea what is going on, but you do know you do not feel right. Most people who experience this kind of thinking also have a sinking feeling they are going "crazy." I do not like the use of that word because it implies that people no longer have control. It is also a demeaning word that destroys the self-esteem of people. However, if something is going on within you and you aren't feeling like your normal self, you must take some immediate action before the problem gets worse and you do end up losing control. The following thoughts may help you realize when you need to take that immediate action:

Confusion: A person who is beginning to have some type of mental health problem will often feel confused or dazed. Concentration ability declines as the confusion grows. This can prove to be the beginning stage of something that could get worse. Seek a medical doctor's help first to make sure there is nothing physical that could be causing your confusion. If there is nothing physically wrong, your medical doctor will recommend that you seek some other type of help.

Despair: Situations often occur in life that can cause a person to feel sad. These are normal reactions to life's stressors. However, when this sadness persists for more than three or four weeks, it is time to take some type of action. Prolonged sadness (depression) can cause thoughts of harming yourself or someone else. Recognize that if your sadness has lasted too long you may be entering into a state of depression. Life's stressors may lead to sadness, but sadness from those stressors is usually transient and a person adapts to overcome these stressors. Depression, on the other hand, may require a person to seek counseling of some type and may lead to a person having to take some form of medication. Depression at its extreme becomes despair. Despair will mean a person may be living without hope. Living without hope can lead to suicide or some form of dangerous behavior when left untreated. There is nothing weak about seeking treatment when it is needed.

Sleeplessness/Sleeping too much: These two symptoms seem to take place in everyone who has a mental health problem. I have counseled people with mental health problems who report these symptoms as being their chief complaint. People living with bipolar disorder often cannot get to sleep because their energy levels are so high. Conversely, people who are experiencing depression often tell me they want to sleep all the time. They have no energy and during the sleep state they do not have to face the depression they experience when awake. Either symptom that is experienced can be dangerous to a person's health. Sleeplessness can lead to a person crashing and to a depressed cycle in people with bipolar disorder. Sleeping too much often leads to a decreased social life, increased social isolation, and deeper depression.

Increased Irritability: If you begin to experience heightened irritability and notice you are a bit grouchier than usual, you should know that something is happening telling you to take action. Even a mild mannered reporter named Clark Kent can be irritable sometimes; however, if that irritability turns worse, it could cause hurt feelings to the ones who love you.

Things do not seem real: If you begin to feel that you are disconnected from yourself or your surroundings, you may be experiencing some signs of a mental health problem. Sometimes it may seem that your hands or some other body part does not belong to you. You may even have a sense of unreality and not be able to discern reality and fantasy.

I am God: If you are having ideas that you have some exaggerated power over other people or your surroundings, you are experiencing some type of mental illness. Many people who experience this type of thinking may think of themselves as God, Jesus, or some super human being with mystical, magical powers. This is often referred to as delusional thinking by those who work in the psychiatric community.

Paranoid Thinking: Sometimes people with a mental health problem will become fearful or suspicious of others. They may also think other people are "out to get them," If you begin to experience this type thinking, please seek immediate help.

Avoidance: Should you begin to avoid people or uncomfortable situations, this can be a signal to you that something is happening and you need to gain some control over it. You may lose interest in other people and avoid being around them. This is a type of withdrawal which can lead to further social isolation, loneliness and even more depression.

Bizarre Behavior: If you start exhibiting behavior that is uncharacteristic of you and behavior that is unacceptable by the norms of the society in which you live, you need to take some action for yourself. See a professional counselor. Talk with someone you can trust who is not judgmental. Learn to control your actions while around other people.

Thoughts of suicide: If you have reached this point in your thinking you have not sought help and have let things go too long. However, it is still not too late to get help. Suicidal thoughts and behavior that could lead to self-harm or violence toward someone else require immediate attention. Do not delay. Get help now. Life is worth living.

Unexplained Physical Problems: If you are having numerous physical ailments that your doctor cannot find an obvious cause, you perhaps should ask for a referral to a psychiatrist. When people cannot handle the problems that occur in everyday life, often these will appear as some type of physical malady. These can be stress related or have some psychological origin. These type problems may manifest as continued pain in one or more areas of the body, tiredness, weakness and numerous other symptoms. After your general practitioner has examined you and cannot find a logical cause, it may be best to seek treatment beyond a physical diagnosis.

Extreme Highs or Lows: One particular mental health diagnosis known as bipolar disorder will manifest in a person with extremely happy feelings one day and extreme depression the next. The high feelings are termed as "mania." While in a manic episode a person may engage in dangerous behavior. Be careful if you are experiencing this kind of behavior. Until you can learn to recognize and control your extreme highs and lows, a doctor may recommend some type of medication to help control your moods. The most common form of medication for this type behavior is Lithium. Many psychiatrists these days prefer prescribing Depakoate for bipolar disorder. Either medication works, but has side effects. See the individual medication's warning label for those side effects and report them to your physician if you experience any of them.

There are other signs and symptoms which can let you know when something is going wrong with you mentally than those I've listed. If you feel something is wrong, by all means, find a doctor and get treatment. It's important that you do this early to avoid your symptoms worsening and leading to some type of inappropriate behavior and subsequent hospitalization.

Impossible Mission?

Mental health systems and programs are only as good as the people who work in them and who administer them. Present mental health systems are failing miserably in regards to teaching people with mental problems to become independent, productive citizens who believe in themselves and their capabilities. It is no wonder that one in four people will be diagnosed with a mental illness this year alone, Out of that fifty-five million people in the United States who succumb to mental illness this coming year, the percentage of those who will bounce back from it is going to be low. It's going to be low because the disparities which exist in the present systems will become despair for those in treatment. Those who are in treatment may not always be aware of the disparities, but those disparities exist nonetheless. They may only become aware of them when they are faced with the coercion, the brow beating, and the downright bullying by some of those professionals who will be treating them for their mental illness.

I am aware that not all mental health professionals behave in this manner. I do not behave this way myself and I work with other professionals who do not. However, there are those who do and to those who do I only hope they are never one of the four who will experience mental illness this year. If they do have to live through this terrible disease, they will become acutely aware that I am not blowing smoke through my ears. I am genuinely concerned about the state of mental health treatment within the United States of America. I am concerned because I believe all people should be treated with dignity and respect. I am also concerned because I am a former mental patient who has lived through some of the disparities you have read about in this work. I am further concerned because tax payer money is supporting some of the nonsense I have seen and experienced.

Is change for the present mental health system in America an impossible mission? I don't think it is. However, I do think it will be an extremely long process before mental health treatment will become the type of treatment that will be benevolent to those people who are known as "the mentally ill." Even the words "the mentally ill," are discriminatory and do not show to those who experience this kind of problem that we think of them as human beings. The change that must take place before mental health systems are benevolent must begin before those who work in mental health ever become "professional." It must take place in the minds and the hearts of people who regard others with a mental problem as inferior or different. The change must begin in the universities where professionals are taught. The change must start with a different mindset than is presently held.

At one time I had the unique experience of living in Russia for four months. Everyone I knew dreaded me leaving the United States and venturing so far from home to a country that was once considered our enemy. However, I found in that country and among the customs of those people, that people are people wherever you travel. My mindset changed within a few days of settling down in the apartment where my wife and I lived. Prejudice can fade. It may not disappear for a long time, but it can begin to fade. The present mindset held toward those who experience a mental health problem can also be changed.

For the disparities to begin to fade away, state legislatures must begin to realize how important funding is needed for more recovery-oriented mental health care. If we do not want people in state hospitals, if we want people to become productive tax-paying citizens, then money must be ear-marked to promulgate recovery – not on programs that don't encourage a person to move forward in life. Certainly not on programs that do not encourage a person to find life and to move away from the mental health system. We have enough of those type programs.

Change is not impossible. It is not impossible for those who live with a mental health problem. It is certainly not impossible for mental health systems to begin to heal themselves either.

www.ingramcontent.com/pod-product-compliance
Lightning Source LLC
Chambersburg PA
CBHW060436290526
45791CB00002B/958